Date

My Nurse Anesthetist Journal

Date
My Nurse Anesthetist Journal

_____ Date

My Nurse Anesthetist Journal

Date ———————
My Nurse Anesthetist Journal

_____ **Date**

My Nurse Anesthetist Journal

Date

My Nurse Anesthetist Journal

My Nurse Anesthetist Journal

Date _____
My Nurse Anesthetist Journal

_____ Date

My Nurse Anesthetist Journal

Date ———————————
My Nurse Anesthetist Journal

_____ **Date**

My Nurse Anesthetist Journal

_____

_____

_____

_____

_____

_____

_____

_____

_____

_____

_____

_____

_____

_____

_____

_____

_____

_____

_____

Date
My Nurse Anesthetist Journal

_____ Date

My Nurse Anesthetist Journal

Date _____
My Nurse Anesthetist Journal

My Nurse Anesthetist Journal

Date _____
My Nurse Anesthetist Journal

My Nurse Anesthetist Journal

Date _____
My Nurse Anesthetist Journal

_____ Date

My Nurse Anesthetist Journal

_____

_____

_____

_____

_____

_____

_____

_____

_____

_____

_____

_____

_____

_____

_____

_____

_____

_____

Date

My Nurse Anesthetist Journal

Date _____

My Nurse Anesthetist Journal

Date

My Nurse Anesthetist Journal

My Nurse Anesthetist Journal

Date

My Nurse Anesthetist Journal

_____ Date

My Nurse Anesthetist Journal

_____

_____

_____

_____

_____

_____

_____

_____

_____

_____

_____

_____

_____

_____

_____

_____

_____

_____

_____

_____

_____

Date _____
My Nurse Anesthetist Journal

_____ **Date**

My Nurse Anesthetist Journal

Date

My Nurse Anesthetist Journal

My Nurse Anesthetist Journal

Date

My Nurse Anesthetist Journal

_____ **Date**

My Nurse Anesthetist Journal

Date

My Nurse Anesthetist Journal

Date _____

My Nurse Anesthetist Journal

Date

My Nurse Anesthetist Journal

_____ **Date**
My Nurse Anesthetist Journal

_____

_____

_____

_____

_____

_____

_____

_____

_____

_____

_____

_____

_____

_____

_____

_____

_____

_____

_____

Date

My Nurse Anesthetist Journal

_____ **Date**
My Nurse Anesthetist Journal

Date

My Nurse Anesthetist Journal

_____ **Date**

My Nurse Anesthetist Journal

_____

_____

_____

_____

_____

_____

_____

_____

_____

_____

_____

_____

_____

_____

_____

_____

_____

_____

_____

_____

_____

_____

Date ———————
My Nurse Anesthetist Journal

Date _____

My Nurse Anesthetist Journal

Date

My Nurse Anesthetist Journal

_____ Date

My Nurse Anesthetist Journal

_____

_____

_____

_____

_____

_____

_____

_____

_____

_____

_____

_____

_____

_____

_____

_____

_____

_____

_____

_____

_____

Date

My Nurse Anesthetist Journal

My Nurse Anesthetist Journal

Date

My Nurse Anesthetist Journal

_____ Date

My Nurse Anesthetist Journal

Date _____
My Nurse Anesthetist Journal

_____ Date

My Nurse Anesthetist Journal

Date _____
My Nurse Anesthetist Journal

Date _____

My Nurse Anesthetist Journal

Date

My Nurse Anesthetist Journal

Date _____

My Nurse Anesthetist Journal

Date _____
My Nurse Anesthetist Journal

_____ **Date**

My Nurse Anesthetist Journal

Date

My Nurse Anesthetist Journal

Date _____

My Nurse Anesthetist Journal

Date _____
My Nurse Anesthetist Journal

_____ **Date**

My Nurse Anesthetist Journal

Date _____
My Nurse Anesthetist Journal

_____

_____

_____

_____

_____

_____

_____

_____

_____

_____

_____

_____

_____

_____

_____

_____

_____

_____

_____

_____

_____

_____ Date

My Nurse Anesthetist Journal

Date _____
My Nurse Anesthetist Journal

My Nurse Anesthetist Journal

Date _____
My Nurse Anesthetist Journal

_____
_____
_____
_____
_____
_____
_____
_____
_____
_____
_____
_____
_____
_____
_____
_____
_____
_____
_____
_____

My Nurse Anesthetist Journal

Date

My Nurse Anesthetist Journal

My Nurse Anesthetist Journal

Date ———————
My Nurse Anesthetist Journal

My Nurse Anesthetist Journal

Date

My Nurse Anesthetist Journal

My Nurse Anesthetist Journal

Date _____
My Nurse Anesthetist Journal

_____ **Date**
My Nurse Anesthetist Journal
_____

_____

_____

_____

_____

_____

_____

_____

_____

_____

_____

_____

_____

_____

_____

_____

_____

_____

_____

_____

_____

_____

_____

_____

Date

My Nurse Anesthetist Journal

Date

My Nurse Anesthetist Journal

Date ———————————
My Nurse Anesthetist Journal

_____ Date

My Nurse Anesthetist Journal

_____

_____

_____

_____

_____

_____

_____

_____

_____

_____

_____

_____

_____

_____

_____

_____

_____

_____

_____

_____

_____

_____

Date

My Nurse Anesthetist Journal

Date

My Nurse Anesthetist Journal

Date ———————————
My Nurse Anesthetist Journal

Date

My Nurse Anesthetist Journal

Date

My Nurse Anesthetist Journal

_____ **Date** _____

My Nurse Anesthetist Journal

Date

My Nurse Anesthetist Journal

My Nurse Anesthetist Journal

Date ——————————
My Nurse Anesthetist Journal

Date _____

My Nurse Anesthetist Journal

Date
My Nurse Anesthetist Journal

Date

My Nurse Anesthetist Journal

Date

My Nurse Anesthetist Journal

My Nurse Anesthetist Journal

Date

My Nurse Anesthetist Journal

_____ **Date**
My Nurse Anesthetist Journal

Date _____
My Nurse Anesthetist Journal

_____
_____
_____
_____
_____
_____
_____
_____
_____
_____
_____
_____
_____
_____
_____
_____
_____
_____
_____
_____

Date _____

My Nurse Anesthetist Journal

Date _____
My Nurse Anesthetist Journal

Date

My Nurse Anesthetist Journal

Date

My Nurse Anesthetist Journal

_____ **Date**

My Nurse Anesthetist Journal

Date

My Nurse Anesthetist Journal

Date _____

My Nurse Anesthetist Journal

Date _____
My Nurse Anesthetist Journal

My Nurse Anesthetist Journal

Date
My Nurse Anesthetist Journal

_____ **Date**

My Nurse Anesthetist Journal

Date

My Nurse Anesthetist Journal

_____ **Date**

My Nurse Anesthetist Journal

Date _____
My Nurse Anesthetist Journal

Date _____

My Nurse Anesthetist Journal

Date

My Nurse Anesthetist Journal

My Nurse Anesthetist Journal

Date

My Nurse Anesthetist Journal

Date _____

My Nurse Anesthetist Journal

Date

My Nurse Anesthetist Journal

My Nurse Anesthetist Journal

Date _____
My Nurse Anesthetist Journal

_____ **Date**

My Nurse Anesthetist Journal

_____

_____

_____

_____

_____

_____

_____

_____

_____

_____

_____

_____

_____

_____

_____

_____

_____

_____

_____

_____

_____

_____

Date _____
My Nurse Anesthetist Journal

_____

_____

_____

_____

_____

_____

_____

_____

_____

_____

_____

_____

_____

_____

_____

_____

_____

_____

Date _____

My Nurse Anesthetist Journal

Date _____
My Nurse Anesthetist Journal